GROWING  GOD

Kerry Walters

GROWING GOD

A GUIDE FOR SPIRITUAL GARDENERS

paulist press new york/mahwah, new jersey

The Publisher gratefully acknowledges use of the following: an exerpt from
The Portal of the Mystery of Hope by Charles Péguy, translated by
David Louis Schindler, Jr. Copyright 1996. Used by permission of
Wm. B. Eerdmans Publishing Co.

Library of Congress Cataloging-in-Publication Data

Walters, Kerry S.
Growing God : a guide for spiritual gardeners / Kerry Walters.
p. cm.
Includes bibliographical references.
ISBN 0-8091-0543-8
1. Spiritual life—Christianity. 2. Gardening—Religious aspects—Christianity.
3. Gardeners—Religious life. 4. Sower (Parable) I. Title.

BV4596.G36 W35 2001
242—dc21
2001050070

Published by
PAULIST PRESS
997 Macarthur Boulevard, Mahwah, New Jersey 07430

www.paulistpress.com

The production editor and book designer was Joseph E. Petta.
The jacket designer was Cynthia Dunne.
Interior clipart images are from eyewire.com.

Printed and bound in the United States of America

For Kathleen Walsh

a good gardener

They, the good soil, my loose and well-cultivated soil.
My well-developed soil.
My good healthy soil of souls, well plowed by my Son for
      centuries of centuries.
Truly, says God, my Son made me some very good gardeners.
They are good gardeners.

Charles Péguy, *The Portal of the Mystery of Hope*

Contents

Introduction

The Secret Garden

We are wont to forget that the sun looks on our cultivated fields and on the prairies and forests without distinction. They all reflect and absorb his rays alike, and the former make but a small part of the glorious picture which he beholds in his daily course. In his view the earth is all equally cultivated like a garden. Therefore we should receive the benefit of his light and heat with a corresponding trust and magnanimity.

Henry David Thoreau, *Walden*

The Kingdom of God is a secret garden.

In the beginning, while still innocent, our Edenic ancestors dwelt in that garden and marveled at its splendor, even though they didn't quite appreciate what they had. Then came the dreadful day when the garden was lost and our parents driven over its borders.

"Roam the world," Yahweh told them. "Scrabble around in the dust for awhile and think about what you once had. Remember the ripe fruit and sweet grasses as you toil and sweat. Maybe then you won't take them for granted. One day you'll be ready to reenter the garden. When you are, here's something for you to chew on: You never really left it. It was inside you all along. The only thing you ever had to do was open the gates of your heart and walk through them."

Growing God

And so our ancestors wandered, baffled by Yahweh's words and haunted by vague memories of a time when the earth was fresh and young. But more was forgotten than remembered with the passing of years, and the secret garden remained hidden. Occasionally spring breezes carried the distant fragrance of soft rain on rich soil. But spring is an all-too-brief season, and year after year the waiting seed was buried in summer dust and entombed in winter ice.

Then one day a strange man walked out of the shadows of history to lead our ancestors—and us today—back to the hidden garden. He came from the fertile hill country of the Galilee, a land with good earth and bountiful crops. This man had discovered the secret garden in his own heart, and he came to announce its abundance and praise its beauty so that the rest of us might regain the Kingdom as well.

Many people jeered when he spoke of the garden, writing him off as a buffoon. But others listened with trembling eagerness and amazement, for his words caressed something deep within their souls. "Teach us,

Rabboni!" they cried. "We've made messes of our lives! Help us to become whole again. Heal us! Lead us out of exile back to the promised land!"

The man struggled to find words to convey to them the great truth that they already possessed the promised land, that the point wasn't to race frantically in a dozen different directions but rather to stand still long enough to see it.

And one afternoon, he found the words.

He stood on the banks of the Galilee's great harp-shaped sea, looking at the freshly ploughed fields that terraced down to its shore. Here and there groves of fragrant eucalyptus trees dotted the landscape. Yellow acacias bloomed. A kingfisher wheeled in the sky, intoxicated by the spring air.

The man shifted his gaze to the crowd of people from Capernaum and Bethsaida who had followed him down to the sea to hear him teach. "It's now or never," he thought. He got into a boat and rowed out a few yards. Standing up, his feet planted firmly on either side of the boat, he called out to them.

Growing God

Listen! A sower went out to sow. And as he sowed, some seed fell on the path, and the birds came and ate it up. Other seed fell on rocky ground, where it had not much soil, and it sprang up quickly, since it had no depth of soil. And when the sun rose, it was scorched; and since it had no root, it withered away. Other seed fell among thorns, and the thorns grew up and choked it, and it yielded no grain. Other seeds fell into good soil and brought forth grain, growing up and increasing and yielding thirty and sixty and a hundredfold....Let anyone with ears to hear listen! (Mark 4:3–9)

The people who stood on the shore were puzzled by his words. What was the Rabboni getting at? His language was familiar enough. After all, people from the Galilee were well acquainted with the ups and downs of spring planting. But his meaning was—and is, still today—mysterious for those not ready to hear it.

Yet the man's words are of the utmost importance, for in this little parable about the sower, he did three things. He reminded us of the secret garden, the Kingdom of God forever seeded away in our hearts. He hinted at how to find the garden. And in telling about the good

6

seed that falls on all the earth, he sprinkled seeds of his own, seeds that will grow into an unimaginably rich harvest if we but cultivate them with persevering trust and magnanimity. Then the earth will yield up its promised fruit and every heart will rejoice.

In short, the man from Galilee told us how to grow God.

This little book is a user's guide to the spiritual horticulture practiced and taught by Jesus the gardener.

Chapter One

Breaking Ground

[We had to] clear the land for cultivation.... We cut and hauled brush, felled a few pines, and tried to pull out roots and rocks with chains....I had never worked this hard in my whole life. By the end of the workday, I ached all over. My hands developed calluses and blisters....Despite these complaints, though, the project was more satisfying and the rewards more immediate than anything I could imagine.

Terry Silber, *A Small Farm in Maine*

The secret garden of God's Kingdom is within you: This is what Jesus tells us in the parable of the sower. Its seeds have already been sown in the depths of the heart. The trick is to allow them to germinate and spring forth.

Anyone who's ever planted a small flower or vegetable patch in the backyard knows how important it is to work the soil properly. The earth must be broken, harrowed, and aerated. Stones and roots that can hinder the growth of seed have to be pried up and carted away. Grubs and cutworms that can wound seedlings must be tracked down and routed. Only then will the garden flourish.

But how to go about tilling the soil of the heart to make it more receptive to heavenly seed? How does one work it so that God may blossom? How does one grow God?

The answer Jesus gives us is this: *Akouete! Listen! He who has ears to hear, let him hear!* Listening is the preliminary chore necessary for spiritual gardening—listening, first, to the parable itself, and then to the mysterious stirring of the seed in the heart to which it awakens us.

If we loosen the soil by listening, anything is possible. If we don't, nothing is.

Gardening Tip #1

The first step in growing God is making your soil receptive to seed. This is best done by listening.

2208   2208

2208

plants with
Bible

Breaking Ground

Jesus' story of the sower and the seed is one of only two parables found in all three synoptic gospels (the other is the parable of the mustard seed). There's also a version of it in the noncanonical Gospel of Thomas, one of the Nag Hammadi scrolls discovered in Egypt in 1945. Although the four texts differ slightly, they all agree in essentials. There's little doubt that the story was actually told by Jesus and passed down by word of mouth until finally recorded sometime around 70 C.E.

A parable is an oddity for those who value straightforward communication, thrive on hard facts, or prefer their information from the printed page. A parable communicates but does so in an indirect and often quicksilverish fashion, is more concerned with deep meaning than factual data, and is better heard than read. This accounts for why so many of us today are tempted to skim over Jesus' parables whenever we run across them in scripture. They tend to strike us as either barely nourishing or frustratingly elusive. In the first case, we grumble for more solid fare, something fillingly meaty to sink our teeth into, not quaint hors d'oeuvres about sowers and seeds. In the second, we find ourselves impatiently wondering why Jesus doesn't just come out and say what's on his mind. We want helpful information about how to get right with God, and all we get are teasing allusions.

Our dissatisfaction with parables arises in large part because we've forgotten the difference between head-knowledge and heart-insight, a distinction more familiar (and more honored) in the ancient world where Jesus lived and taught than in our own.

Head-knowledge is factual information communicated directly and rationally. The language proper to it is pared down to nonallusive description and step-by-step explanation. This is as it should be. When we bake a cake, travel, serve on a jury, or labor through a technical manual, we want clear information and unambiguous directions. They help us to get the job done.

But heart-insight is a horse of a different color. An insight is a sudden flash of recognition, an intuitive "Aha!" that discloses truth that a lockstep fidelity to mix-and-stir directions can't. Head-knowing operates in a steadily cumulative fashion: We climb succeeding tiers of evidence and arguments until we arrive at a conclusion. But insight, when it comes, is a swift penetration to the heart of the matter that bypasses normal routes of rational inference.

Knowledge can be taught (otherwise any type of schooling would be quite beside the point, wouldn't it?), but not insight. It can be evoked through story or poetry or song, but never learned in the way we might learn history or science. In studying such disciplines, we energetically reach out with both hands to grab facts and bank them in our intellectual safety deposit boxes. But the appropriate strategy for receiving insight is a patient waiting and silent listening that encourage grateful receptivity.

Put another way, knowledge is an acquisition that adds to our store of information; insight is a gift that transforms our very being. Knowledge makes us well-informed. Insight makes us well-fulfilled.

Now, a parable is an evoker of insight, and a particularly sly one at that. On the surface, it appears to convey mundanely factual head-knowledge. It uses simple language and describes scenarios that the listener easily recognizes: how to plant a crop properly (Mark 4:3–8), how to be a good shepherd (Luke 15:4–6), how to bake bread (Matt 13:33). If interpreted as just an instructional squib on commonplace chores, nothing could be less illuminating than a parable. Folks in first-century Palestine had no need of a prophet to lecture them on planting, herding, or baking. Those of us today, who buy our vegetables and bread from supermarkets and only run across sheep when we count them on sleepless nights, are in even less need of such instruction.

It eventually dawns on all but the very dullest of listeners, then, that the words of a parable must mean more than they literally say. So it is with the parable of the sower. "Sower," for example, can't *just* refer to an actual husbandman, any more than the words "seed" or "soil" *merely* stand for grain or earth. They point to more profound referents and aim to provoke the perplexity that leads first to wonder and then insight.

This is the beauty of a parable. It nudges us to look beneath the surface of conventional objects and familiar activities and see them in a new light. It teases us toward the realization that the commonplace we so often take for granted shimmers with deep meaning and hidden promise. It aims for insight: literally, for a recognition of profound truth hidden away *in*side the ordinary, a secret so difficult to communicate that it eludes the frontal assault of head-knowing. This doesn't mean we throw over reason when responding to a parable, but rather, as the Greek fathers were fond of putting it, that we allow the head to sink into the heart.

In this regard, Jesus' parables work along the same lines as the koans of the Zen Buddhist tradition. Koans, like parables, are stories that describe down-to-earth objects and situations in such disturbingly novel ways that our usual canons of interpretation blow apart. Knowledge's reliance on collecting and analyzing information is no help here. How does logic help one understand bizarre koanic utterances such as "In the trees fish play, in the deep sea birds are flying" or "On top of a flagpole a cow gives birth to a calf"?

The obvious answer is that it can't, and this is precisely the lesson a koan wishes to convey in a memorably startling way. As one commentator puts it, koanic utterances "reveal to us the inherent limitations of the logical mind as an instrument for realizing ultimate Truth. In the process they pry us loose from our tightly held dogmas and prejudices." Our familiar ways of viewing the world and our place in it collapse, clearing the ground for a new look and a fresh start.

A parable operates in the same fashion. The Hebrew word for parable, *mashal*, suggests a riddle or mystery that takes us past the ordinary. The Greek even more explicitly points to the koanic function of a parable. "Parable" is derived from the combination of the prefix *para*, "beyond" or "alongside," and the verb *ballein*, "to cast" or "to throw." A parable is a riddle that works with or alongside conventional meanings to catapult us beyond them into a new level of awareness—into insight.

When we hear a parable, we're invited, as Jesus said (Mark 4:11), to partake in a *musterion*, or mystery. In its New Testament sense, a *musterion* is a secret teaching that appears boringly commonplace to an outsider—that is, to the head-knower who takes the words of a parable literally. But to someone who enters into the *musterion*, follows its lead, and patiently listens to what it has to say, it offers life-changing truth. What the poet Wallace Stevens once wrote of art is even more applicable to parable: Its "wonder and mystery" lie in the fact that it's a "revelation"—an insight—of something "wholly other" than what one would've expected from a surface glance at it. And in receiving that revelation, the recipient is forever transfigured.

So, what's the *musterion* in the parable of the sower?

Atypically, Jesus offers a gloss on his own parable (Mark 4:14–20). He tells us that the seed in it symbolizes the "Word" or *logos*. The parallel text in Luke (8:11) is more specific: The seed is the "Word of God," *logos tou theou*. This Word is sown in the soil of the human heart. Once there, it languishes or flourishes depending on how the heart responds to it. One possibility is that the heart refuses to acknowledge the Word, and it lies dry and unproductive on the sun-baked path. Another is that the heart initially thrills to the Word but quickly loses its fervor, thus preventing the Word from becoming deeply rooted. A third is that the heart is too preoccupied with other matters to concentrate on growing the Word properly, and it soon suffocates in a dense thicket of thorns. The final possibility is that the heart heeds the Word, nurtures its growth in receptive soil, and grows the secret garden.

Jesus' use of a seed to symbolize God's Word is especially evocative. Seeds are repositories of life, tiny powerhouses of creative vitality. They're the sources of being, containing within them the nature and destiny of that into which they will grow if properly tended. In Hebrew scripture, the divine Word is described as the fecund seed from which all creation springs: The Word is planted in the void, and everything that is comes into being (Gen 1:1–3). In Christian scripture, the creative Word that seeds reality is the Christ. John tells us that Jesus is the nutritive "Word of life" (John 1:1) that animates all creation. Revelation says that Jesus is the

Word of God (19:13), and Paul calls Jesus the "Wisdom of God" (1 Cor 1:24), with "Wisdom" or *sophia* closely connected in meaning to "Word" or *logos.*

The message in both Hebrew and Christian scripture is that reality is seeded with the generative presence and power of God—what New Testament authors called "grace." The divine Sower beneficently casts himself with both hands upon the void, and reality suddenly is. Each and every being that springs from this original throwing of seed likewise contains the germ of divine creativity within it. God the Sower is not totally distinct from either the seed or the secret garden that springs from the seed. The seed bears the vitality of the Sower, and so does the fruit. God spreads the seed of life, of being, and in doing so plants himself. God sows Godseed. Grace.

Jesus' parable reminds us that we're called to care for the Godseed sown in our heart so that we might both share and nurture the fullness and creativity of God. Jesus the Word, Jesus the fully grown Seed, is the living example of what it means to accept the gift of being. In him, the potential for growth divinely planted in us is completely realized. Be like me, as I am like the Father, said Jesus. Quicken the Godseed sown in you from the beginning of time. Grow into your humanity by growing God. Be good gardeners.

If we open our hearts, this is the *musterion*-insight given us by the parable of the sower.

But as the parable reminds us, seed requires proper soil-care to germinate. God supplies the seed—himself—yet it's up to us to till and tend the ground. And that ground is us. A human—*homo*—is *humus*—earth. If we neglect cultivating the "pastureland of the heart," as the fourth-century monk Pseudo-Macarius called it, we cannot grow the good seed and discover the secret garden. It lies dormant on the heart's stony path, or it finds too little earth to sink roots, or it germinates only to be choked by thistles and briars. The invitation to be is rejected, the growing season squandered, the garden lost.

The upshot is doubly tragic. We remain brutish clods rather than branches of the vine we're meant to be. Even worse, we rob God of his opportunity for growth in and through us. Meister Eckhart, the fourteenth-century preacher and mystic, once said that God needs us even as we need God. Jesus hints at the same conclusion in his parable of the sower. Without good seed, soil is barren. But without receptive soil, seed cannot grow.

This brings us back to listening, the first step in growing God.

Listening's initial task is attunement to the *musterion*-message hidden in the parable of the sower itself. This insight breaks the surface of the ground.

But merely turning the sod over isn't enough. One must dig more deeply to loosen the soil and prepare it for fruitfulness. The earthly gardener works the broken soil so that seed has elbow room to germinate and push upward. The spiritual gardener must do the same thing by putting her ear to the ground and focusing all her attention on the throbbing presence of Godseed in the loam of her heart. This second, more profound kind of listening crumbles the clay of delusion and distraction that impedes the secret garden's growth.

We can get a better handle on listening by turning to theologian Karl Rahner, one of this century's master gardeners. Rahner's message is that the listening that grows God is really a remembering. Embedded with Godseed as we are, each person already contains the promise of harvest within his or her heart. But we generally forget its presence to such an extent that it takes a special effort to recall to consciousness what we knew all along. When we cultivate the soil by listening, we remember.

Gardening Tip #2
Listening is remembering.

Breaking Ground

According to Rahner, all finite human experience is ultimately "grounded" (a particularly good choice of words for a discussion of growing God!) in what he calls a "pre-apprehension" or intuition of the Absolute: God. Although this pre-apprehension is "ever-present," it lacks the sharp quality of "some definite, particular objective thing which is experienced alongside of other objects." Instead, the pre-apprehension of God silently hovers in the "background" of consciousness as a kind of "secret ingredient." But for all that, it determines the horizon of each and every one of our experiences. "It is a basic mode of being which is prior to and permeates every objective experience."

Rahner's reason for claiming that a pre-apprehension of God is the background of our experience lies in the simple (but at the same time boggling) fact that humans are creatures who question. To question is to move beyond or "transcend" the here-and-now and project oneself into new places and different times. It is to envision and move toward possibilities that stretch the given "facts" of any situation in creatively novel directions.

Growing God

Moreover, these possibilities are infinite. As Rahner says, "Every answer is always just the beginning of a new question." One question leads to another, one emergent possibility flows into a whole set of new and unexpected ones, and this forever "situates [us] in a broader horizon which looms before [us] in its vastness." When we tune into this, we experience ourselves as "infinite possibilities"—creatures not totally bound by either accident of birth or fluctuations of history. We know ourselves as the incredibly creative beings we are, because our questioning allows us to go beyond what we seem to be at any given moment.

It takes but little reflection to realize that the infinity of possibilities our questioning reveals gestures at something other—and greater—than ourselves. We are but creatures, and that means we're not absolute. So our ability to experience an infinity of creative possibilities points to an *absolute* reference point to which we're related without fully sharing its absolute nature, a reference point we're always dimly aware of. And this is God. God the Sower is the absolutely creative Being who grounds infinite possibility; the Godseed he strews in the soil of our hearts allows for the pre-apprehension of God that haunts all our experience; and this pre-apprehension is attested to by our creative ability to question.

So because of the Godseed planted within us—those nuggets of creative vitality that reflect God's ultimate creativity—we're born with a "background" intuition of God. The trick is to make contact with this intuition so that we can grow it into full consciousness. Spiritual cultivation of our *humus* requires making the effort to listen to the deep stirrings of Godseed and thus remember who we are.

Jesus aims to evoke this recollection in the parable of the sower. It's a necessary reminder because all too many of us exist in a state of chronic forgetfulness. We become so distracted by other concerns in our journey through life that we cease listening to what we ought to. We vaguely sense the infinity of our possibilities, but fail to recall their true meaning, interpreting them as opportunities for fame or wealth or power instead of for growth into and of God. When we stop listening we cease remembering, and Godseed lies dormant. As a consequence, our soil remains unreceptive and our lives barren. The secret garden of God's Kingdom eludes us.

But the listening that awakens remembrance works the soil so that the good seed may grow.

Gardening Tip #3
Remembering is openness.

We can conclude from all this that the listening that elicits remembrance is a radical opening of one's heart to the creative Word graciously implanted within it.

We've seen that for earthly seed to flourish, the ground in which it's planted must be cleared. Brush and overgrowth have to be removed, stones and debris hauled away, entangling roots chopped. Only then will the seed have the open space it needs. Similarly, Godseed requires soil free of impediments to growth. The *humus* we are must be cleared, raked clean of everything that blocks our ability to remember the Word, harrowed of the debris that prevents us from growing our pre-apprehension of God into full consciousness. To be open is to become a clearing, a pristinely open piece of land capable of growing the infinite possibilities seeded away in us.

In Rahner's language, the radical openness that clears the soil of our hearts is made possible by our questioning. We stand in the midst of the bramble-cluttered and thistle-choked fields our lives have become. As we survey the terrain, two choices confront us. We can either shrug our shoulders and accept our fruitlessness as an inevitability—"This is just the way things are, and there's nothing I can do about it!"—or we can ask ourselves some hard questions: "Who am I?" "What am I?" "What do I want out of life?" "What *should* I want out of life?" "Is it just possible that the field that I am might bear more worthy fruit?"

Growing God

The moment we start to ask these sorts of questions, we call ourselves *into* question. The very instant that happens, we plunge a shovel into the sod, upturn the earth of our hearts, and begin to listen for answers. We move beyond the here-and-now to hearken to the Godseeded possibilities within us. The present no longer seems inevitable. We now recollect, even if only vaguely and inarticulately, that we're much more than we appear to be, that there's great promise locked away in us crying to be liberated. We sense that things need not remain the way they are, that we need not weep by Babylon's waters forever. This thrilling insight, born of the self-questioning fueled by our pre-apprehension of a reference point infinitely greater than ourselves, steadily opens us up to the fecund possibilities that are ours. And as we stand in the wild and forlorn field, thistles and briars give way to the vision of a gemlike garden full of greenery and running water.

When we question, we begin to listen. When we listen, we start to remember. And when we remember, we open to the wonderful grace-possibility that unfolds before us—the prospect of growing God and dwelling in the secret garden. Then the soil of the heart becomes a clearing ready to nurture the good seed.

This is the *musterion,* this is the heart-insight, extended to us in the parable of the sower. Little wonder that Jesus prefaces his gardening advice with the command *Akouete!*

Chapter Two

Surviving Drought

High temperatures which usually accompany summer droughts deplete the supply of soil moisture.

M. G. Kains, *Five Acres and Independence*

A seasoned gardener is both confident and humble. She knows there's much she can and ought to do to nurture seed. As we just saw, the first and foremost thing under her control is ensuring that the soil is receptive to growth. But a good gardener also foresees that certain happenstances over which she simply has no control may interfere with the growth of her crop. She accepts this, patiently bowing to their inevitability.

One of these is weather. The wise gardener realizes that every growing season is subject to the whims of weather. She's savvy enough to anticipate that at some point or other her carefully cultivated seed will have to endure parching spells of heat and drought. She can't prevent these inclemencies, but she can learn to adjust to them. And indeed she must, for the future of her garden depends on how well she does.

So it is with growing God. When the *musterion* Jesus offers prods us first into questioning our commonplace assumptions about who we are and then into listening, remembering, and opening, the soil is loosened so that Godseed may germinate. But we would be rash—as well as arrogant—to suppose that the secret garden will spring up without complications. Heart soil is subject to weather shifts that, although generated by the sorts of creatures we are, really are out of our control. We may fancy the garden is well on its way and all our worries over. But drought will inevitably descend upon it. Then, as Jesus told us, our carefully cleared soil will bake hard and dry as a well-trodden clay path. There's nothing we can do to ward off the burning winds and blazing sun. But we can acknowledge them as inescapable facts and steel ourselves to endure when they come.

Gardening Tip #4

Be forewarned: Climate isn't under your control. Drought will occasionally hit the garden through no fault of your own. So learn something about weather patterns to prepare for the arrival of dry spells.

After all the labor it takes to till the soil of our hearts, it may seem terribly unfair that we have to put up with intermittent droughts that threaten the growing season. But this is just the way things are, and it's foolish to waste time protesting the inevitable. It's far more sensible to spend one's energy trying to understand why the dry spells hit in the first place. Then, hopefully, one can get through them.

Karl Rahner has already hinted at why spiritual droughts afflict us. Recall what he said. A human is a strange composite of finitude and infinity, subject to time and place on the one hand, yet uncannily seeded with traces of the limitless Absolute on the other. These traces account for our innate pre-apprehension of God as well as our ability to call the present into question. But they don't negate the fact that we're still situated in concrete conditions that render us relative rather than absolute. We *can* transcend or go beyond any given here-and-now. But we must do so as children of the earth rather than as angels free-floating in the heavens.

What this implies, as author C. S. Lewis noted some sixty years ago, is that we're "amphibians—half spirit and half animal."

> As spirits [we] belong to the eternal world, but as animals [we] inhabit time. This means that while [our] spirit can be directed to an eternal object, [our] bodies, passions, and imaginations are in continual change, for to be in time means to change.

Our amphibian nature—one foot in the eternal, the other in time—makes us susceptible to what Lewis calls the Law of Undulation. "Our nearest approach to constancy," he says, is "the repeated return to a level from which [we] repeatedly fall back, a series of troughs and peaks." Sometimes the eternal side of our nature comes to the fore, and we exult on the peak of God-nearness. Then Godseed flourishes and the garden grows. But at other times our temporal side breaks through, and we catapult into an imprisoning trough of all-too-human God-estrangement. Given what we are, this back-and-forth undulation is a "natural" and inescapable phenomenon.

It's in the trough periods that spiritual drought sets in. Our pre-apprehension of God fades in the sizzling sun, our enthusiasm for gardening dries up, and all our initial work in tilling the *humus* seems so much wasted time and energy. The sproutlings that have begun to poke their heads through the soil droop. But the heat and dryness so sap our spirit that we just don't give a damn. Let 'em wilt. Gardening was a stupid idea anyway.

The spiritual dryness that periodically besets us was well known to our ancestors. Qoheleth in the Book of

Ecclesiastes suffers from a surfeit of it when he laments that "all things are wearisome; more than one can express; the eye is not satisfied with seeing, or the ear filled with hearing. What has been is what will be, and what has been done is what will be done; there is nothing new under the sun" (1:8–9). In the Book of Revelation, the Laodicean church is rebuked for its dryness: it is neither hot nor cold, but tepidly indifferent, and the Lord abominates such lukewarmness (3:15–16).

In the first centuries of Christianity, the desert mothers and fathers likewise endured the downswing of spiritual dryness. They called it *acedia,* from the Greek for "does not care," or *taedium cordis,* "heart-weariness." They also frequently referred to it as the "noontide demon" because it assailed its victims with a torpor and sickness of heart every bit as enervating as the blazing noon sun. When it hits, as the desert hermits told John Cassian in the fifth century, it either benumbs the soul with indolence or crushes it with a despairing sense of futility. Years later, Geoffrey Chaucer observed in "The Parson's

Tale" that *acedia* makes a person heavy-hearted, peevish, slack, slovenly, and despondent.

Every Christian has suffered through the heat wave of *acedia*—including, I suspect, Christ himself during his great wilderness testing. It's not the same thing as doubt. The person assailed by the noontide demon isn't undergoing a crisis of faith. She continues to believe in God. It's just that she couldn't care less. Spiritual matters that once gladdened her heart and quickened her pulse now leave her indifferent. All this talk about God and soul and the Kingdom of Heaven at best weary her, at worst strike her as insipid and irrelevant. Prayer is burdensome, spiritual reading offputtingly saccharine, Mass tedious. All she wants is to lie somewhere in a shady patch and forget the whole dreary business.

What's especially alarming about *acedia* is that it strikes without apparent warning, and there seems no way either to inoculate oneself against it before it hits or dose oneself with a pick-me-up after it's come. One day we're working in our gardens, content with God and the world, eagerly gauging the growth of our seedlings. The next we awaken with such a sense of sluggish disgust for gardening that we can barely get out of bed, much less muster the energy to actually pick up our hoes. Nor does there seem any escape. Even if we had a spiritual cure-all in our medicine cabinet, we lack the resolve and interest to go fetch it. Why bother? Who cares?

So we sit and blink as the scorching wind blows through our souls, dries and drifts our carefully tended *humus*, and bakes the good seed on the heat-cracked paths of our hearts.

There's neither a vaccination nor a cure for *acedia*. We can't control the weather. Droughts come when they will, and they depart the same way. But the spiritual gardener ought to keep in mind two points. The first, hard as it may be to swallow, is that droughts are opportunities. The second is that even though we can't prevent or remedy dry seasons, there *are* strategies for getting through them until the rains return.

Gardening Tip #5

Believe it or not, dry spells make for good gardens—and, eventually, for good gardeners as well. They test and strengthen the soil, and they don't—they *can't*—harm the seed. The seed is untouchable.

The secret garden that aches to blossom forth in our hearts is nothing less, as we saw in chapter 1, than the Word incarnating itself. From the beginning of time, the Word seeds all creation with its vitality so that one day creation might be luxurious with the green presence of the Divine. This is God's great gift to us: the gift of being, the possibility of growing God so well that we become replicas of him, children of the New Adam, aglow with the shimmering presence of God. When that wondrous day of fruition finally arrives—the great *parousia*, or homecoming, as theologians say—the Kingdom returns.

Growing God

But the gift of being, no more than any other kind of gift, can't be crammed down the recipient's throat. It must be accepted wholeheartedly and gratefully. The response must match the caliber of the gift: freely given to bestow life, freely received and joyfully lived, not taken for granted or plumped into a drawer to be pulled out only on special occasions. Put another way, the gift is genuinely received only when the recipient consciously wills to so make it the centerpiece of his existence that he and it become indistinguishable. Then God's gift of God is truly accepted, and the seed embedded in our *humus* comes into its own.

When we amphibians are riding our peak periods, the gift seems easy to accept. Swept away by enthusiasm and zeal—what Theresa of Avila called "sweet consolations"—we tuck it in our pockets and shout hosannas. But this doesn't necessarily mean we've responded in the manner the gift deserves. We may be taking it for granted, sucking on it with the smug cockiness of a spoiled child who believes he has an unlimited supply of lollipops.

Surviving Drought

So periodically God pulls back a bit and allows us to slide into the trough of *acedia*. It's not that the gift of being is taken away. Once planted, Godseed is always ours, regardless of how foolishly we cultivate it. Nor is it the case that God withdraws to browbeat or blackmail us into loading him down with supplications or abasing self-accusations. Toadyism isn't his idea of a healthy relationship. Instead, he pulls back to allow us to test our commitment to the gift. Only when our backs are against the glaring white wall at high noon can our mettle be appraised. Only when we no longer bask in the glow of the gift's sweet consolations can we discover whether we've truly accepted it.

Droughts, then, are opportunities for insight into the depth of our commitment to spiritual gardening. But they're also much more than that. They're regimens that strengthen our soil. C. S. Lewis puts it like this. When God withdraws "supports and incentives,"

> He leaves the creature to stand up on its own legs—to carry out from the will alone duties which

have lost all relish. It is during such trough periods, much more than during the peak periods, that it is growing into the sort of creature He wants it to be.

Despite appearances to the contrary, spiritual gardeners are never more productive than when "no longer desiring, but still intending" to do God's will—than when, in short, they "look round upon a universe from which every trace of Him seems to have vanished," and still obey.

Gardening Tip #6
When you hoe—hoe!

Here's a Zen parable for you. A frazzled disciple, wilted by the noonday glare, goes to his master for advice. "Sensei!" he pleads. "Counsel me! I no longer have any hunger for enlightenment. Tell me what to do!" "Have you a garden?" the master asks. "Yes." "Then go hoe it!" "But what about enlightenment?" says the puzzled disciple. *"Forget enlightenment!"* the Sensei roars. *"When you hoe—hoe!"*

This is sage advice for anyone languishing in a dry season, and it accords squarely with Jesus' recommendation to his own disciples that they concentrate on the present moment and forget their cares about the morrow (Matt 6:25–34). Simply do what needs to be done, concentrating as best you can on the task before you, trying to forget memories of past enthusiasm as well as presently jaded dreams about the future. Pick up your gardening tools and set to work. Your mind and soul aren't in it; the noontide devil has seen to that. Very well. There's nothing to be done about that. But the demon can't prevent you from forcing your body to go through the mechanical motions of gardening, even though your heat-exhausted spirit longs to plop down in the shade and forget everything.

Just hoe.

This may be unsatisfying advice for those addicted to "self-improvement." Surely there must be something "proactive" we can do to jolt ourselves from the dry season's doldrums, to wrest control and bootstrap out of *acedia*. But take time to consider: What could we possibly do? The trademark of spiritual dryness is losing the very *desire* to grow God. Self-improvement strategies only make sense if we *wish* to improve, and the gardener suffering from *acedia* can't even work up the energy to long for a cure. The most he can do is grit his teeth and resolve to get through the business at hand, hoeing his rows without looking to either the right or the left, the past or the future.

Even though this may not seem like much, it's really a great deal. Hoeing is a kind of listening in itself, a hopeful listening that both tests our long-term commitment to gardening and strengthens our resolve. Hope for what? For resurrection, as St. Paul reminds us (1 Cor 15:14,17). Resurrection of what? Resurrection of the desire for God. Resolute hoeing is hoping that the drought will pass and that we will once again experience the *frisson* of growing God, of standing in our tilled and tended gardens and thrilling to the sight of green sprouts. All this goes on beneath the surface, of course. At the conscious level, hoeing in the midst of *acedia* is a crushingly wearisome and apparently futile job. But deep down, where it really counts, our hopeful listening bears fruit. The soil responds to the rhythm of the hoe. So does the seed.

There's another reason why the proper response to spiritual dryness is hoeing. Occupying ourselves with a task, even a tedious and seemingly stupid one, gets us through the day. Time lies on the heart like a heavy weight during the dry season. Everything stands still under the noon sun. But forcing oneself to go through a routine, however deadly it may seem at the time, takes our mind off the vacuum into which we've been sucked. It redirects our focus away from the killing glare to the immediate necessity of moving steadily down the first row of sproutlings, up the next, down the next, and so on. Before long, one becomes nothing more than the ever-present act of hoeing, and this absorption in a mechanical task is precisely the proper therapeutic response to drought.

Growing God

The desert monks knew this well. A story is told about the Abbot Paul, a man especially susceptible to the noontide devil. For years he sweated and languished under the demon's assaults. Then he discovered how to hoe. He collected palm leaves, sat in his cell, and day in and day out wove them into baskets. At the end of each year, he would sell some, give others away, and burn the rest. Then he would collect more palm leaves and begin all over again.

Paul did this not because there was an actual need for the baskets, but "simply for the sake of purifying his heart, and strengthening his will, and persisting in his cell, and gaining a victory over *acedia* and driving it away." He was wise enough to realize that sometimes in spiritual gardening the only thing one can possibly do is grab one's hoe, woodenly chop away at the dry clods, and wait for the advent of rain.

Hoeing isn't just hopeful listening. It's also a waiting, even though the parched gardener may scarcely remember what it is she awaits. But the very fact that we're capable of waiting under such hostile conditions underscores the great mystery C. S. Lewis has already brought to our attention: We're closer to the secret garden during our trough periods than we can know. In one of his sermons, theologian Paul Tillich explains why:

> ...although waiting is *not* having, it is also having. The fact that we wait for something shows that in some way we already possess it. Waiting anticipates that which is not yet real. If we wait in hope and patience, the power of that for which we wait is already effective within us. He who waits in an ultimate sense is not far from that for which he waits. He who waits in absolute seriousness is already grasped by that for which he waits. He who waits in patience has already received the power of that for which he waits.

Those of us who labor in God's garden, those of us who at times can do nothing but force ourselves off the dusty ground to hoe, will discover the same thing good Abbot Paul did—the waters *do* return to a dry heart. When they do, and if we've faithfully persevered in our listening and waiting, our gardens will be in good order.

Growing God

Therefore, take to heart what the holy Father Zossima of Dostoyevsky's *The Brothers Karamazov* says:

> ...there is no need to be troubled about times and seasons, for the secret of the times and seasons is in the wisdom of God, in His foresight, and His love. And what in human reckoning seems still afar off, may be Divine ordinance close at hand, on the eve of its appearance.

Chapter Three

Fertilizing

Take it easy on all types of fertilizers. Too much manure can cause as much trouble as any other kind of fertilizer.

Walter L. Doty, *All About Vegetables*

There's one gardening strategy I find particularly distressing, although I confess I've used it in bygone days. It's called "forcing," a name whose bellicosity is entirely appropriate.

This is how it's done. You take the bulb of a flower such as a narcissus or a tiger lily or an amaryllis. You plant it in a small pot of soil that's been fertilized to the max; this is especially important. Then you bombard the bulb with artificial heat and light, and shower it with out-of-the-ordinary amounts of water. If things work the way they're supposed to, the intense environment creates a hothouse effect that forces accelerated growth. In quick order the bulb sprouts, stalks, and blossoms. Almost before you know what's happened, a beautiful flower is born.

Growing God

Forcing is most often done in the bleakly gray winter, when our hearts so ache for a bit of color that we simply can't bear to wait for spring. The upside of forcing is a quick payoff. But rushing a seed in this way exacts a terrible price. Both soil and bulb are so overworked by the forced growth that they become exhausted. The blossom is splendid for a few short days, but then quickly fades and wilts. The fertilizer that quick-stepped the bulb to fruition can't sustain the spurt, nor will the small amount of potted soil allow the bulb to sink deep roots.

The practice of forcing reminds me of Jesus' warning in the parable of the sower. Some Godseed springs up overnight because its soil is too richly, too greedily, fertilized. But the heady growth is so unnaturally rapid that it drains vitality, and the sproutlings soon languish with exhaustion. We can kill in our rush to grow God.

Impatiently forcing Godseed is an ever-present temptation, especially right after coming out of a dry spell. We feel an urgent need to make up for lost time, to bring forth the Kingdom *now*. So we shovel on the fertilizer in the hopes of collapsing an entire growing season into a

Gardening Tip #7
What's important is solidly rooted
growth, *not* quick growth.

few short days. Bad move. "For everything there is a season, and a time for every matter under heaven" (Eccl
3:1), and the march of the seasons, just like the coming
and going of the weather, bends to no one's will.

Religious merchandisers entice the gardener with any
number of quick-growth products. Some of them are
quite exotic fertilizers, marketed to appeal to those with
an adventurous spirit. Others are old-fashioned manures,
aimed at gardeners who conservatively desire a more
"natural" or "organic" approach. In and of themselves,
none of these products need be pernicious if judiciously

57

Growing God

applied. The problem arises when we begin to dump them on our seedbeds with extravagant abandonment.

The top-selling exotic fertilizer is miracle-growth enthusiasm. The most popular organic manure is magic-growth piety. Each comes with detailed application instructions, and each promises quick return on the gardener's investment.

By *enthusiasm*, I intend the meaning given the word by early eighteenth-century speakers. In their lexicon, *enthusiasm* connoted a religiosity characterized by intense affect. For the enthusiast, the hallmark of being right with God is an emotional frenzy that violently wrenches him out of the mundane realm to kerplop him willy-nilly before the celestial throne. (*Enthousiasmos*, the Greek word from which we derive "enthusiasm," in fact means being "possessed" or "taken over" by the gods.) The enthusiast avidly seeks an explosive rush of religious passion, accompanied of course by predictable symptoms: profuse tears, bodily tremors, spontaneous recoveries from physical illnesses, gibbering in tongues, fainting fits, and a near-sexual exultation.

Fertilizing

Some leaders of charismatic and revivalist movements, Protestant as well as Catholic, specialize in dispensing the exotic fertilizer of miracle-growth enthusiasm. Harvey Cox refers to them as modern-day "circuit preachers" who "travel by jet instead of on horseback" to whip up "the once-saved and the would-be-saved." They offer a strange blend of traditional fire-and-brimstone warnings and New Age-inspired strategies for salvation: "psychodynamics, primal scream, basic encounter, rolphing, body awareness, bioenergetics and techniques for inducing joy, openness, enhanced feeling."

The sellers of miracle-growth aim to whip emotions to such a white heat that Godseed "miraculously" breaks through the soil and surges upward with all the dizzying speed of Jack's beanstalk. The accelerated growth is painful. The devotee is buffeted with violent emotions that cannot but bruise him. But curiously this fisticuff approach also brings a nearly unbearable delight to the enthusiast. For him, emotional pain and pleasure are so closely intertwined as to be inseparable. They symbolize the breaking through of the miracle he demands.

Growing God

The manure of magic-growth piety promises quick results in a different way. Gardeners who prefer it find the laser show of miracle-growth enthusiasm unseemly. They prefer something less flashy and high-tech, something more "organic." But for all that, their goal is the same: a spiritual jumpstart so powerful that it forces the quick maturation of Godseed.

Magic-growth piety operates under the assumption that there are tried and tested incantations, formulae, and ritualistic observances that the gardener can invoke to ensure the swift growth of her sprouts. Like the druids of old who threw bones and chanted harvest spells under waxing moons, users of magic-growth believe there's great juju in meticulous conformity to popularly pious practices. So they supplement their gardens with extravagant doses of incantatory prayer and ritualistic wizardry, confident that the magic liberally strewn about guarantees growth spurts.

A sobering example of magic-growth's organic manuring comes from my own local newspaper. Periodically in the classified ads section there appears a "Prayer to the Blessed Virgin," always submitted anonymously, that promises quick results—"never known to fail!", the announcement assures readers. The prayer is to be said three times for three consecutive days as the supplicant concentrates on the problem she wants fixed. "After three days," we're assured, "the request will be granted. This prayer must be published after the favor is granted." A three-day growing period isn't quite as dramatic as the immediate results promised by miracle-growth enthusiasm, but it's good enough—and a lot less unsettling. It hasn't the side effects of fainting or twitching.

The spiritual gardener should stay away from both of these fertilizers—or, at the very most, use them sparingly. The prudential rule here is "less is better." No one can reasonably deny that the prospect of growing God's Kingdom fills the heart with emotions of joy and longing, and that Godseed is nurtured by both of these. Neither should we casually pooh-pooh conventional piety's appeal to set prayers and ritualistic observances. Such regimens can encourage the self-discipline and steadfastness needed to cultivate a garden for the long haul. So it would be churlish as well as arrogant to dismiss religious affect and popular piety out of hand.

But it's a different story when the two are used to force quick growth out of Godseed. Then they become gimmicks that give us short-term satisfaction at the expense of draining our soil of its vitality.

Intense religious emotion takes us to the heights of empyrean ecstasy. But emotional flare-ups, like all combustions, soon sputter. After the revival tent comes down and the circuit rider moves on, the effulgent dame's rocket that shot up with the help of miracle-growth burns itself out. The growth spurt has been misdirected, shunting energy toward the blossom when the place it's really needed is underground, in the roots. The resulting top-heaviness means that the plant sooner or later collapses under its own weight. It simply hasn't the solid root system needed for sustained growth.

Magic-growth piety brings the same sad fate. Scrupulous recitation of a magical prayer three times for three successive days fills us with an empowering sense of accomplishment. We actually see the garden growing right before our imagination's eyes. Anticipation swells, visions of fulfillment buoyantly shimmer in front of us. As each rote recitation is faithfully ticked off, we can feel energy snowballing in the direction of fruition. Then the day when the wizardry is supposed to take hold arrives. Generally, of course, nothing spectacular happens. And because our energy was overly concentrated toward outward growth rather than inward root structure, it fizzles in disappointment and perhaps even an enraged sense of betrayal. The fertilizer winds up poisoning rather than enriching.

Gardening Tip #8

When it comes to growing God, there are no fast lanes or short cuts. Fertilizers that promise otherwise should generally be avoided.

Growing God

These dismal consequences should be kept in mind as we wonder about what fertilizers to apply to our gardens. One thing is certain: Impatience never brings good harvests.

Forcing Godseed into hypergrowth by laying on massive amounts of fertilizers and manures is obviously motivated by our impatience for results. What may not be obvious, however, is that impatience is a child of distrust. When we resort to miracle-growth and magic-growth gimmicks, we do so because we fundamentally distrust the divine promise that the secret garden is already here and now, and that all we have to do to enter into it is open the *humus* of our hearts.

That impatience springs from distrust can be better appreciated if we reflect on other situations where we impetuously rush events. In conversation with a slow or stuttering speaker, we jump in and finish her sentences. When working with our kids on science or art projects, we elbow them aside and take over. At the office, we throw ourselves on a mountain of work without taking the time to delegate any of it to someone else.

Frequently we try to cast a good light on these actions with self-serving excuses: "I knew what she (the stutterer) wanted to say. I was just trying to help her along"; "The project was dragging on and he (the child) was getting tired and cranky. I thought it best to finish up quickly"; "If you want a job done well, do it yourself. Besides, everyone else (coworkers) already has a lot on their plate."

But these excuses are pretty transparent, aren't they? What really motivates our impatience is distrust: "This woman isn't capable of speaking for herself, so it's up to me to finish her sentences"; "My kid will screw up the project if left on his own. I better take over"; "Those clowns at the office botch everything they touch, so I'll have to tackle the job myself." Embedded in this kind of distrust is a deep arrogance. The distrustful person considers himself superior to the object of his distrust. He's more competent, better qualified. So why suffer fools gladly?

Such distrust is bad enough when directed toward our fellow humans. But it's especially pernicious in spiritual gardening, because its underlying assumption is that we're more competent than God to take care of business. Sure, God sows the seed. Yeah, yeah, of course Jesus promises that the seed will bring forth fruit if it lands in good soil. But let's shove things along some, just in case God's a little overworked or a tiny bit preoccupied at the moment. Let's give the poor guy a hand. Let's get the ball in play.

And so we pile on our fertilizers and manures.

Gardening Tip #9
The best fertilizer for Godseed
is trust.

A good gardener appreciates that a seed planted in well-prepared soil can be relied on to do what it's supposed to do. A seed, remember, is a cell charged with life, a powerhouse of creative vitality aching to break forth and give birth. Seed is wise. It carries its own set of instructions. The seed knows what's best for it, and the wise gardener follows its lead with trust and patience.

The birthing of sprouts from seed must follow the natural rhythm defined by the seed's encoded instructions. Forced acceleration of the gestation period tries to second-guess these instructions. This in turn leads, as we've already seen, to the misdirection of energy from inward to outward growth that gives rise to beautiful but transient blossoms.

So it is with Godseed. The secret garden is sown in the heart of every person. But the seed willingly accommodates itself to the temperament and talents of each individual. It knows that some hearts require a longer growing period than others; that some hearts are prone to drought; and that some hearts are clogged with greater deposits of clay and gravel than others. The divinely encoded instructions for growth adjust themselves accordingly.

Growing God

When we care for the Godseed implanted within our hearts, we can do no better than fertilize it with the trust that it knows those instructions better than we. The thing is not to assume that the seed needs a kick in the pants because the garden isn't springing up overnight as we wish. Likewise, we must resist the temptation to compare the growth curve of our garden with those of our brothers and sisters. Their soil is not ours.

Instead, humbly acknowledging that Godseed knows what it's up to, we must gently cooperate with it by bending our wills to its rhythm rather than insisting on setting the timetable ourselves. We must trust the seed enough to let it alone.

Gardening Tip #10
Trusting is letting-alone.

Fertilizing

To trust is to permit the object of trust to go at its own speed, even if the pace it chooses isn't fast enough for our liking. When we trust, we forego pushing our personal schedules forward. We give way because we believe that the other's schedule is better, even if different, than our own. More to the point, we patiently work within the parameters of that schedule.

We let it alone to take its own time.

The letting-alone that comprises the essence of trust has two related senses, both of which have already been implied.

In the first place, letting-alone means *not intruding upon*. Trusting entails holding back one's impetuosities and allowing the trusted object to do what it does naturally. In the second place, letting-alone means *positively assenting to*. To trust is to accept the object of trust's schedule, to follow its lead, and to cooperate in its coming about.

In the language of scripture, trust is faith: the willingness to believe that "things not seen" are nonetheless present and silently at work for one's own good (cf. Heb

11:1). Faith in the power of Godseed to grow into the secret garden; faith that the growth rate of Godseed has been ordained by One wiser than we in these matters; faith that holds us back from trying to speed things up; faith that there's ample time for the garden to flourish without our frantic forcing: this is what it means to let the seed do *what* it does *when* it wants to do it.

When we have faith in Godseed's wisdom, we get out of its way by resisting the temptation to rush its growth. Miracle-growth fertilizers and magic-growth manures remain on the store shelf or compost heap where they belong. The only fertilizer we should use is the only one we need: our willingness to patiently let the seed grow as it should, to accept that Godseed's sense of time isn't necessarily ours, and to nevertheless say yes to it so that the secret garden—and we—might be.

When you think about it, trusting Godseed in this way really recapitulates on a much smaller scale the manner in which God trusts us. God doesn't bombard us with fertilizer. He refuses to coercively pull us up by the ears and force our growth, although he certainly could if he wished. Instead, he gives us all the time we need, standing to one side to allow us to grow in our own way toward him, but also graciously collaborating, ever so gently, in that growth. He takes a chance on us—humans are "God's risk," as the theologian John Macquarrie wisely says—because he has enough faith in our gardening abilities to leave us alone. When we grow God in the secret garden, we can follow no better example than the one God himself gives. Fertilize gently with trust so that the roots are left alone to sink gradually and deeply into the heart's *humus*, so deeply that they can never be wrenched up, so deeply that they push their way downward to the virgin soil of eternity.

Chapter Four

Pruning

*A common cause of failure in the vegetable garden is too many
kinds—too many experimental plantings, instead of the garden being devoted to the things we know and like. We lose
much of what makes a garden worth having by not efficiently
controlling the thoughtless and harmful mania for mere size.*

Mme Vilmorin-Andrieux, *The Vegetable Garden*

Many gardeners find pruning and weeding especially vexing.

I'm one of them. It's not so much that I mind the work. Pruning, after all, isn't as labor intensive as digging the soil of one's garden, and it's certainly less taxing than swinging one's hoe during dry spells.

No, the truth of the matter is that pruning gives me the emotional willies.

My intellect tells me that a healthy garden is an uncluttered garden: Sproutlings need room to breathe and stretch their muscles if they're to thrive. That means a garden shouldn't be overloaded with a multitude of different specimens, and that the occasional wind-borne seed that finds its way into the garden and sends up shoots ought to be culled. Otherwise, what one intended to grow risks being choked by all the competition.

But my emotions tell me something else. They tingle with excitement at the mere sight of growing things—not only my planned crop, but adventitious wildflowers and even weeds as well. Each of these squatters radiates green life, and it seems somehow wicked—or at best callous—to rip them up by the roots and toss them on the compost pile. My first impulse is to nurse them into chaotic fruition as carefully as I would any other sproutling—and, just as foolishly, to add to the jumble by running out and buying even more seeds to plant.

But when it comes to gardening, more simply isn't better (a lesson already underscored by the last chapter's discussion of fertilizing). We spiritual gardeners must steel ourselves to forego going crazy with seed catalogs and to prune with determination any and all sproutlings that might please our sense of novelty but hamper the growth of Godseed. If we don't we thwart our aim of growing God. As Jesus warned, the Godseed will be stymied and possibly suffocated by the overcrowding.

Gardening Tip #11

The secret garden in which God grows isn't an overgrown jungle. Don't allow it to become one.

And this means, of course, that we lose our squeamish reluctance to cut back and prune whenever and wherever we should. Not everything that *can* grow in a garden *should*.

There are any number of reasons why we balk at pruning our gardens. Like me, we may resist because we've no stomach for it. Or we may be neglectful out of sheer laziness or greed or vanity. In the first case, we simply don't make an effort to keep the garden tidy. We convince ourselves that it'll grow on its own anyway and that when harvest time comes there will be enough of a crop scattered among the weeds to sustain us. In the second case, we conclude that a good garden is defined by variety rather than quality. So we stubbornly refuse to cull undergrowth in any way. We not only hoard every weed and bramble that springs up, we also add to the mess by planting all sorts of exotic seeds: theological seeds, denominational seeds, guru seeds, pop spirituality seeds. In the third case, our mania is driven by old-fashioned vanity: We want our gardens to be more impressive than anyone else's. We want to win blue ribbons.

Other reasons for failing to prune can be more subtle. Sometimes we high-mindedly tell ourselves that our refusal to trim back is really a benevolent concern for our neighbors: We want our gardens to overflow so that at harvest we'll have a surplus of crops to give away. At other times, we overplant and underweed because of spiritual timidity: We fear that some catastrophe (such as drought) may overtake the garden, and we hope that letting *every*thing grow rampantly will ensure that at least *some*thing survives.

But the consequence of each of these moves proves identical: The garden becomes a jungle, and adventi-

Pruning

tious plants crowd and shade the Godseed shoots. At the end of the growing season, we may have a wildly luxuriant garden filled with all sorts of flamboyant blossoms and fruits. But God won't be one of them.

Troublesome as laziness, greed, vanity, confused generosity, and timidity are, an even more insidious reason explains why so many of us overplant and underweed our gardens: bored restlessness. This malaise is so pervasive that I suspect it's the single greatest cause for gardens exploding into jungles. Georges Bernanos grippingly captures it in a passage from his novel *The Diary of a Country Priest*:

> [T]he world is eaten up by boredom. To perceive this needs a little preliminary thought: you can't see it all at once. It is like dust. You go about and never notice, you breathe it in, you eat and drink it. It is sifted so fine, it doesn't even grit on your teeth. But stand still for an instant and there it is, coating your face and hands. To shake off this drizzle of ashes you must be for ever on the go. And so people are always "on the go."

Gardening Tip #12
A messy garden most likely points to a bored gardener.

Although the two are frequently confused, boredom isn't the *acedia* of dry spells. Far from it, as a matter of fact. The noontide devil saps the gardener of energy and initiative. All she wants to do is find a bit of shade and go to sleep. But boredom isn't a soporific. It's an amphetamine, a high-voltage hit of speed, a rush of adrenaline. The problem with a bored person is that she's unable to channel her energy. It's diffuse and directionless, sending her scurrying all over the map in short-lived flurries of activity. She's looking for something to throw herself into wholeheartedly. But because her pent-up nervous energy is undisciplined, she never calms down long enough to focus and commit. Consequently, as Bernanos says, she's perpetually "on the go," frenetically searching for the latest thrill or escapade or cause. To be bored is to be pierced through and through with a restless and painful discontentment.

When it comes to spiritual gardening, boredom drives the gardener, as Mme Vilmorin-Andrieux says in the epigraph to this chapter, into a "thoughtless and harmful mania for mere size"—and, I might add, increasingly exotic variety. Despite her initial good intentions, the bored gardener simply can't stick with the most important task at hand: growing God. After a few weeks of focused listening her concentration begins to break. The old restlessness reasserts itself, and she's on the prowl for a new activity to throw herself into. She feverishly blueprints additions to the garden: an arbor here, a pond over there, a few fruit trees, maybe a cactus corner. Then she flips through seed catalogues and races from one greenhouse to the next in search of rare and novel cuttings to carry back to her garden.

These new projects consume her for a while. She feels as if she's finally found what she's looking for. But inevitably the bite of boredom gnashes her, and she scrambles to find a new, more exciting—more "promis-ing"—venture. Her garden becomes a chaotic jumble of half-completed and then deserted projects, so cluttered with the ruins of her restlessness that there's barely room to breathe, much less walk.

And what of Godseed? Its cultivation falls into the sad disrepair characteristic of all the bored gardener's short-lived projects. One distraction after another gets in the way of tending it, and the sprouts it sends up become lost in the ever-thickening jungle. The seed, mind you, doesn't die; Godseed is immortal. But the shoots that spring from it can wilt out of neglect and the sheer press of surrounding overgrowth.

When we complain of boredom, what we generally *suppose* we mean is that our lives are empty. Think of the bored kid on summer vacation from school who gripes that "there's nothing to do!" This lament usually astounds and irritates her parents to no end. "What do you mean, 'nothing to do'?! You've got plenty of possibilities! You can read, visit friends, play sports, go swimming...!", and so on.

The summer doldrums of a schoolchild, as well as our earlier discovery that restlessness is the root cause of boredom, clue us into a truth that typically goes unnoticed. The bored person isn't impoverished of possibilities. On the contrary, she's inundated with them. Far from being empty, her plate is too full. And that's the problem. She's overwhelmed with so many possibilities that she can't figure out which are worth committing to and which can be sidelined. The moment she tries to focus on one, others entice her. Then the restless hopping from one to the next starts.

Recall Rahner's suggestion in chapter 1 that to be human is to be blessed with an infinity of possibilities. Our awareness of these possibilities should nudge us toward God, their absolute source.

But sometimes, when we fail to listen and remember, we overlook the deep meaning our possibilities point to. We read all of them in relative terms, supposing that they gesture at nothing more than the short-term options immediately facing us. These options are numerous, and many of them seem so appealing that we can't decide between them. So we scurry from one to the other, furiously trying to grab as many as we can. Our bustling about robs us of the time and calm to consider two points: first, that the only reason any *relative* possibility attracts us to start with is because it reflects the supremely attractive *absolute* possibility of growing God; second, that some of our relative possibilities are more worthy of pursuit than others precisely because they aim more directly at God-growth.

If we miss these two points, it's little wonder that restlessness sets in and the overplanted and underpruned garden becomes a jungle. Attending to the primary possibility of growing God gets sidetracked by our bored clutching at less important ones. Distractions pile up so high that the Godseed sproutlings get lost in the tangled undergrowth. In order to avoid this unhappy situation, we must identify the plants most essential to our garden and devote all our care and attention to them.

Gardening Tip #13

A good gardener is single-mindedly committed to the growth of her main crop This requires discernment, discernment births love, and love is the antidote to the restlessness of boredom.

If we would grow God successfully, we must discern which possibilities are essential and which extraneous to our garden. Having done that, we can't help but lovingly dedicate ourselves to the essential, even if it means pruning back the extraneous.

We begin to discern by learning how to recognize which of the possibilities that appeal to us are *genuinely* desirable.

We're attracted to a possibility because we find it desirable. This seems obvious enough. Moreover, anything that seems desirable to us does so because it strikes us as good. We do not—we *cannot*—desire an object we judge as other than good. No reasonable person desires what will harm him.

But simply desiring something obviously does not guarantee its goodness. We can be and frequently are mistaken about what's genuinely good and hence genuinely desirable. When this happens, we make bad choices that damage us in the long run, even if they seem satisfying enough at the time. So it's crucial not to confuse what's desirable because good with what we fancy is good only because we desire it.

When considering all the gardening possibilities to which we're attracted, then, we need to ask ourselves which are desirable because *truly* good. And we find the answer to that question by realizing that the genuinely good, and hence the genuinely desirable, draws us closer to our heart's deepest longing: the secret garden, the Kingdom of Heaven. Every molecule and cell in our bodies ache for a recovery of the full being promised by God. This is our true good, the purpose for which we were made, the absolute end to which all our relative possibilities ultimately point.

We achieve this good through the single-minded cultivation of the Godseed sown in our *humus*. We may be distracted along the way by other desirable possibilities: planting exotic orchids and rare cacti, enlarging our gardens to include flora from all over the world, letting the wild flowers that spring up take over the pastureland of the heart. But appealing as these possibilities are, they're not genuinely desirable if the opportunity cost is choking Godseed. Other plants and projects may immediately please our senses or satisfy our vanity. But in the long run they get in the way of the one absolute good for which we yearn: the garden of God. Only in that garden can we *be*, and only in being will we achieve our heart's desire.

When we realize that growing God is the only absolute good, and hence the only absolutely desirable possibility, something wondrous happens to us. We're drawn to that good as a moth to the flame. It irresistibly beckons us. Remember, we're incapable of denying the desirability of what we take to be good, and in this case our judgment is absolutely correct, our discernment right on the money.

This discernment isn't abstractly intellectual. It's not just another bit of knowledge we lock away in our cerebral vault. Instead, it's more akin to the transformative experience of insight—or, better, a reawakening of the initial insight that led us to till the soil of our hearts in the first place. It involves our whole person, heart as well as head, reason as well as affect. The discernment of the absolute good and absolute desirability of growing God settles the mind, eases our restlessness, comforts our yearning heart, and binds our loyalty and commitment. We cease racing around because we've found the one end that ultimately satisfies us.

In short, we move from discernment to love. The bored person, the restless heart, has found nothing worthy to love—in fact, boredom and restlessness are antithetical to love. But love is bound to its object, single-mindedly focused on and fulfilled by the good discerned in it. Love rests, as St. Augustine noted, in what it loves, and neither wants nor needs anything else.

Just as significantly, love takes us out of ourselves even as it satisfies our deepest yearning. When we love the genuinely good and desirable—the genuinely lovable—we ache to ensure its well-being. How could it be otherwise? How could we not want to serve and protect the good once we've finally discerned it? So we concentrate our attention and energy on working for the flourishing of that which we love, first and foremost for its sake, but for our own as well, knowing that the well-being of what we love is a necessary condition for ours, too.

At this point the God-grower overcomes her reluctance to prune and weed the garden. She distinguishes her essential crop from extraneous growth, longs to see it flourish, and lovingly invests heart and soul in helping it do so. She cuts back all the distractions that earlier preoccupied her and interfered with the steady growth of the main crop. She's like the merchant who sold all he had to obtain the pearl of great price. He sacrificed what once commanded his attention to gain something of infinitely greater value. But his goal wasn't mere possession; he also longed to care for the pearl, to honor and revere its absolute beauty.

So it is with the gardener who discerns, and in discerning comes to love, Godseed. She gives up relative, nonessential gardening possibilities, attractive as they once seemed—attractive as they still may be—for the sake of the one absolutely desirable possibility. Orchids and cacti and rose trellises remain things of great beauty and have a place in our gardens. But they are and always will remain secondary in importance to the flourishing of Godseed. Until the growth of God is firmly established in our gardens, they may have to go or at least be cut back—not in a savage slash-and-burn spirit, but in one of tender regret.

When the God-sprouts are well on their way, we can return to the roses and orchids, and maybe even put in that lily pond we once dreamed about. Perhaps we can even allow the wildflowers to come back. But then orchids and roses and ponds and wildflowers will all serve as background embellishments that highlight the majesty of the God-crop, not distract from it. In fact, if truth be told, their beauty will be magnified a hundred-fold, precisely because they now take their proper place in the garden as spokes radiating from the central axis.

That axis, the center of the garden, the center of the world, is also the center of our lives. In resisting the manic temptation to let our gardens run wild, we discover a great mystery. We aren't just gardeners. We're also the fruits of the very garden we tend. In growing God, we too become spokes radiating from his central blossom, borrowing our greenness and beauty from his. Our sap rises as God's rises, and in restoring his garden we restore ourselves. As George Herbert wrote long ago,

> These are thy wonders, Lord of love,
> To make us see we are but flowers that glide:
>   Which when we once can finde and prove,
> Thou hast a garden for us, where to bide.

It's time to consider this greatest mystery of gardening more fully.

Chapter Five

The Enchanted Garden

This very evening, in the dusk, I was walking in my garden alone.... Outside the wall of green made by tall spruces, I heard voices .... I called to the strangers, asking them to enter, to wander where they would. In they came, and we spent a few moments together enjoying the soft sight of many blooming flowers, the sweet scents in the dew, the rich greens of foliage and turf in the fading light; then I left them still exclaiming over the beauty of what they saw....The best wish I can wish for any one is that he may have a garden of his own, a little garden in which, through work and sweet imaginings he may find a creative happiness unknown to those without this dear possession.

Louisa Yeomans King, *Chronicles of the Garden*

When I was a boy, I read a fairy tale, a story about a garden. The garden was a wondrous, enchanted place. Luscious fruit dripped from tree boughs, and the fruit was always within easy reach. Gaily colored flowers and sweetly scented grasses carpeted the ground. The sky was forever blue and light-filled, even (and this was especially splendid!) when soft showers fell to moisten the earth and its growing things.

But rain falling from clear skies wasn't the garden's most marvelous feature. *This* was: Whenever anyone plucked a fruit or flower, another immediately sprouted in its place. The garden magically replenished itself. Its riches were inexhaustible. And so was the happiness of those lucky few who dwelt there.

Growing God

Even as a child, the vision of this enchanted garden broke my heart with longing. In one way or another, I suppose I've been searching for it ever since. Jesus the master gardener, Jesus the spinner of koans and parables, suggests that *all* of us have the same yearning, even though we may not quite be able to articulate it as well as the author of my fairy tale. And he promises that those who seek the enchanted garden will find it.

The fairy tale of my boyhood is nothing less than an attempt to describe what the Kingdom of Heaven is like when we successfully nurture God in our soul-*humus*. In an earthly garden, the growing season eventually plays itself out, the harvest is reaped, and that's the end of it. But in the secret garden that springs from the seeded Word, the fruits are always harvested—thirtyfold, sixtyfold, a hundredfold—yet never exhausted. There, as Edmund Spenser so delightfully tells us,

> Daily they grow, and daily forth are sent
> Into the world, it to replenish more;
> Yet is the stocke not lessened, nor spent,

The Enchanted Garden

But still remaines in everlasting store
As it first created was of yore.

The secret garden hidden away in our hearts blossoms into the enchanted garden, available to each and every one of us, if we make the effort to grow Godseed properly. In opening the soil through listening, waiting out dry spells with hope and loyalty, fertilizing the sproutlings with trust, and giving them room to flourish by pruning with the discernment of love, we make ready a dwelling place for God and for ourselves. Our wandering ends. We come home. And that home sparkles with the promise of enchantment.

Fruit #1
The first fruit of spiritual
gardening is Dwelling.

Growing God

Our forgetfulness of the secret garden turns us into nomads who ceaselessly roam through valleys and over mountains, setting up tents wherever we happen to find ourselves at day's end, breaking camp the next morning to move on. But this wandering existence isn't natural to us. We're creatures who long for a home, some permanent place where we can sink down roots, some haven to call our own. We yearn to dwell rather than wander.

Wandering is a perpetual state of becoming, always on the move yet never arriving. But to dwell is to *be*. Dwelling is arriving.

Recall what we discovered in chapter 1: In the primordial act of sowing, God extended the gift of being to all creation, inviting everything that is to fulfill its destiny and flourish. But humans rejected the gift, and the seeds of being planted in our *humus* entered a long period of dormancy. Each and every one of us vaguely senses their presence in our hearts (this is what Rahner meant by the "pre-apprehension" of God that serves as the background of our experience), but neither the seeds nor we can develop until we start listening to them. The garden remains secret, our true home is hidden from us, and we continue our cheerless nomadic existence.

All that changes when we follow the advice of Jesus the gardener. We till the soil and tenderly care for the God-sproutlings so that their roots may grow deeply and firmly. The sleeping seed awakens, the plants grow, and the forlornly barren steppe on which we once roamed transforms into a welcoming abode, a place to remain. We accept the gift, and in doing so find the stability for which we've longed. We begin to be, and in being, to dwell. Moreover—and this is the greatest mystery of all—so does God.

In growing and dwelling in the Kingdom of Heaven, we flourish into full being.

In flourishing into full being, we fulfill our role in God's original plan, thus helping God to flourish as well.

Think of this grand connection between our well-being and God's in ecological terms. The garden is an ecosystem whose final goal is the flourishing of the whole. But the maximal well-being of each part depends on the maximal well-being of the other parts. If one languishes, it affects the entire ecosystem.

The two main parts of the garden are the human soil and the divine seed. Both depend on the other. The soil needs the good seed's life; the seed needs the nutrients of good soil. When properly cultivated, the soil allows the seed to fulfill its purpose and come into its own. When the seed grows into fruit and flowers, the soil fulfills *its* proper function and thus comes into its own as well.

Moreover, the two enrich one another in the process. The soil that once lay sleeping is stirred into vitality by the growth of the seed, and the once dormant seed is nourished by the receptive soil.

Finally, soil and seed develop such a close relationship of mutual support in the divine-human ecosystem that they interpenetrate one another in an inseparably intimate way. As the seed grows, the soil that served as its hotbed is absorbed into its spreading roots and cells and tissues, into its very leaves and petals. The plant and the soil commingle without quite losing their separate identities, and as they do, they edge closer and closer to the stability and fruition—the being—both are destined for.

When the growth cycle is completed, the Kingdom of Heaven, where God is fully God and humans are fully human, is at hand. Each bestows being on the other, each dwells in the other, and what was once secret is made manifest. The Body of Christ, the divine ecosystem, is complete. And this ecosystem is an enchanted garden, for the fruit it bears never withers and never diminishes. Pluck a flower, and it miraculously reproduces. Tug at a cluster of grapes, and another takes its place. The creative vitality coursing through the garden and binding together God and humans is inexhaustible. God's connection with us, and our connection with God, is forever sustained.

One of the most ancient Christian liturgies that has come down to us, the one recorded in the early-second-century *Didache*, offers this posteucharist prayer: "Thanks be to thee, Holy Father, for thy sacred Name which thou hast caused to dwell in our hearts." I don't think it's too much to suppose that when God the sower hears these words, he responds in kind: "Thanks be to thee, patient and persevering *humus*, for thy care of the sacred Name which I have caused to dwell in thy heart."

Fruit #2
The second fruit of spiritual gardening is Sharing.

One of the great pleasures of earthly gardening is sharing. As Louisa Yeomans King says in the epigraph to this chapter, the successful gardener delights in showing strangers the "many blooming flowers" and "rich greens of foliage" he or she has successfully cultivated. Beauty demands to be shared.

So do bumper crops of fruits and vegetables. At summer's end, the successful gardener takes what she needs

The Enchanted Garden

and gives the rest away. Who among us hasn't delivered sacks of surplus tomatoes, beans, cucumbers, or corn—not to mention the ever-abundant zucchini—to neighbors, relatives, coworkers, food banks, and retirement homes? Those who tenderly and patiently nurture crops throughout the spring and summer months understand that there's something profoundly amiss in letting the fruit of their efforts go to waste.

In addition to beauty and bounty, gardeners share a third thing with others: the wisdom of their experience. Excellent gardeners aren't born with green thumbs. They've gotten where they are through years of hard work and perseverance. They've endured their share of droughts, occasionally overfertilized, ill-prepared the soil at times, foolishly allowed their gardens to run wild at others. But they've learned from their mistakes and gained a finely honed sensitivity to the rhythms of the growing season. Those of us just beginning know we can go to them for sage advice and enthusiastic encouragement.

The sharing that comes so naturally to earthly gardening is multiplied thirtyfold, sixtyfold, a hundredfold, in

spiritual gardening. How could it not? The enchanted garden in which God as well as the soul have their dwelling
place is resplendent with beauty: the beauty of being. The
fruits of that garden abound because the seed from which
they spring is inexhaustibly generative: Pick as many as we
will, the supply never diminishes. Finally, the gardening
expertise picked up along the way—the heart-insight that
brings our background pre-apprehension of God to explic-
it consciousness—so fills and overflows us that it can't help
but splash over into the hearts of our fellows.

Here we discover another level to the *musterion* of
Jesus' parable of the sower: In being called to grow God,
we're also called to grow our brothers and sisters.
Spiritual gardening is never an exclusively solitary enter-
prise; the enchanted garden has no walls around it. The
ecosystem of the heavenly Kingdom is open rather than
closed, and one of the gauges of its health is the extent
to which it spreads to the backyards and pasturelands of
our neighbors.

This means that the spiritual gardener has a commis-
sion to bring as many people as he possibly can into the

enchanted garden so that they too might find a dwelling place there. His growth *of* God has simultaneously been a growth *into* God. Godseed's creative vitality, the Word's always present longing to break forth into fecundity, is now incarnated by the gardener, and its pulsating energy impels him to go forth and serve as a catalyst for the spiritual growth of others. His acceptance of the gift of being chrisms him with the privilege of bearing the gift to others.

This responsibility to others can take many forms, depending on both the talents and temperament of the gardener and the situations and dispositions of those to whom he ministers. Sometimes, harkening back to Rahner's insight, it entails gently coaxing our sisters and brothers to take their human ability to question seriously enough to focus on fundamental rather than relatively frivolous possibilities. At other times, it means inviting them to enter the enchanted garden in which we dwell and take a look at the splendors it offers. Finally, our responsibility to share the gift always means encouraging others to listen carefully so that the *humus* of their hearts can become receptive. It also means offering loving advice and patient hands-on assistance to help them get through dry spells or resist the temptations to overfertilize and underprune once they too begin to grow God.

In short, we're called to share whatever we have that might help others cultivate Godseed in their own plots. Marvelous as the enchanted garden of God's Kingdom is, the good gardener senses that it is somehow incomplete until all his sisters and brothers dwell there with him and God. As the Catholic poet Charles Péguy once asked, how can one truly relish Paradise knowing that some of one's fellows have been left behind?

Fruit #3
The third fruit of spiritual
gardening is Joy.

The Enchanted Garden

I'm forever grateful that Jesus performed his first miracle at a party.

We all know the story. Jesus and his disciples are whooping it up at a wedding celebration in Cana. As was the time's custom, the party had probably been going on for a few days. Everyone was gay and excited; at weddings, as even gloomy Jeremiah conceded (16:9), "the voice of mirth and the voice of gladness" properly fill the tent. Then a vexing discovery was made: The heart-warming wine was all gone. And then the miracle: Rather than have the festivities bust up, Jesus laughingly presented his own wedding gift to the new couple. He turned water into sweet wine. In doing so, he as much as said: Live it up! Be joyful! You were made for joy!

We should all take this tale to heart, for it reminds us of something we're apt to forget: God is joyful and wants us to be joyful too. As the wise Father Zossima we met in an earlier chapter observes, "...men are made for happiness, and anyone who is completely happy has a right to say to himself, 'I am doing God's will on earth.'" John XXIII, that great and good pope who grew God so well in our own time, echoes this sentiment. A "sad" Christian is a "bad" Christian, he was fond of remarking, for "Christianity is peace, joy, love, and a life that is ever renewed."

Spiritual gardening blesses us with the gift of joy or happiness (I use the terms synonymously). As the God of joy grows and thrives in the *humus* of our hearts, as our roots intertwine with his and the divine sap rises to animate our limbs, we partake in the vibrantly happy belly laugh that rings throughout creation. Joy is the third fruit in the enchanted garden, and like everything that grows there, it never diminishes.

How can we better understand the happiness that comes from spiritual gardening? Perhaps the shortest cut is the one mapped by the ancient Greek notion of happiness as *eudaimonia*, an activity and state of the soul in accordance with excellence. According to this way of thinking, we humans have an end or purpose to which we're destined by virtue of the type of creatures we are. This end or purpose is the "excellence" that serves as the ultimate standard of evaluation. When it's achieved, we become everything we're meant to be. We're fulfilled.

The Enchanted Garden

We experience a state of joyful flourishing, and all our activities flow from and express this state. We attain *eudaimonia*.

Now, we've already seen that our proper end as humans entails accepting God's gift of being. When we heed and cultivate the Word seeded in our hearts, we cease our roaming—our restless moving without arriving—and return to the home for which we're destined: the divine garden, the Kingdom of Heaven. Dwelling there *fulfills* us, utterly and inexhaustibly, because it *fills* us, utterly and inexhaustibly, with the flowering presence of God. We are no longer in a state of becoming. We've now arrived, we know who we are and where we ought to be, and we rejoice.

Moreover, our happiness is so exuberantly uncontainable that we, like the celebrants at the Cana wedding, feel the need to gaily dance and to pull others into the dance with us. The joy that comes from achieving the full being we're destined for—the joy that comes from finally experiencing what it means to be completely, totally *alive*—only quickens our desire to share the garden with others so that they too might know the happiness of attaining excellence. And why not? There's more than enough to go around. The fruit of the enchanted garden is inexhaustible.

The excellence of growing into God and arriving at full being, then, brings a thirtyfold return of joy. The exhilarated urge to draw others into that same excellence increases the joy sixtyfold. Nor does the joy stop there. We're promised that cultivating the garden will bring us a hundredfold measure of happiness. And so it does, for in reaching our own destiny, our own excellence, God reaches his as well. God's prospering is mysteriously linked to ours. When we come into our own, so does he. What greater joy can there conceivably be than knowing that our grateful acceptance of the divine gift of being also gifts God with fulfillment? The joy of dwelling in the garden isn't ours alone. It's also God's.

A Final Gardening Tip
The best time of the year
to grow God is
now.

The experienced earthly gardener digs out her almanac in winter's final weeks to remind herself of the last frost date of spring. Where I live, it generally falls between the middle of April and the first of May. Prior to its arrival, gardening is a risky business. Seedlings lovingly planted in freshly turned soil can still be blackened by an overnight cold snap. But if the gardener bides her time until the threat of frost has passed, seed and sprouts will be safe. Then the earth becomes warm and moist, ready to grow whatever's in it.

The spiritual gardener doesn't need an almanac to tell her the right time to begin growing God, because *any* time is right. The growing season is year round. It's always now, at the present moment. The seed has already been planted. Soul-*humus*, by its very nature, contains it. All that's needed to start the miracle of germination is listening. The only garden tools required are hope, trust, and love.

Many of us put off growing God because we suppose the time isn't ripe. We might feel, for example, that we simply don't have the requisite knowledge to garden well. So we let the pastureland of the heart lie untouched while we bone up (depending on our tastes) on arcane theology or pop spirituality. Or we might suppose that our soil is so rocky and acidic that we need landscaping gurus to come in and overhaul the lot. So we waste time by checking the yellow pages for addresses and phone numbers, getting appraisals, and weighing various courses of treatment. Or perhaps we fancy ourselves living in an area whose weather is too dry, or too wet, or too hot, or too cold to grow God. So we stay inside our cozy, climate-controlled houses, promising ourselves we'll take up gardening just as soon as we can move to a more simpatico locale.

112

The Enchanted Garden

But these are flimsy excuses, aren't they? We already have everything we need. What more could an entire library of books teach us? Our *humus* is naturally rich. All it needs is a bit of cultivation, and we're entirely capable of doing that on our own. And Godseed is capable of sprouting in all seasons, even the terrible droughts of *acedia* that occasionally blow in. The wonderful possibility of the secret garden, the Kingdom of Heaven, is *here, now,* just waiting to be allowed to grow. This is the great *musterion* of Jesus' parable of the sower.

A story is told about St. Francis of Assisi. It seems he found himself one icy, gray day on a winter-blasted heath. The only tree in sight was an almond, leaf-stripped and frost-gnarled. Francis put his ear against the almond tree's bark. "Preach to me of God!" he whispered.

And there, on that lonely, frozen heath, the almond tree's white flowers blossomed forth and filled the air with light and fragrance. God grew, even in the dark of winter.

So will God grow for us, whatever the season, if we ask and listen.

O Lord Jesus, true gardener, work in us what you want of us, for without you we can do nothing. For you are indeed the true gardener, at once the maker and tiller and keeper of your garden, you who plant with the word, water with the spirit and give increase with your power. You were mistaken, Mary, in taking him for the gardener of that mean little garden in which he was buried: he is the gardener of the whole world and of heaven, the gardener of the Church he plants and waters here below until, its harvest yielded, he will transplant it into the land of the living by the streams of living water, where it will fear no more the summer heat, where its leaves will be for ever green and it will never cease from bearing fruit. Blessed are they who dwell in your heavenly gardens, Lord, through endless ages will they sing your praise.

Guerric of Igny (twelfth century)

Sources

 CHAPTER 1

"...reveal to us the inherent limitations....": Philip Kapleau, *The Three Pillars of Zen* (Boston: Beacon Press, 1967), p. 64.

"...wonder and mystery....": Wallace Stevens, *Opus Posthumous: Poems, Plays, Prose,* ed. Milton J. Bates (New York: Alfred A. Knopf, 1989), p. 237.

"...pastureland of the heart....": *Pseudo-Macarius: The Fifty Spiritual Homilies and the Great Letter,* trans. and ed. George A. Maloney, S.J. (New York: Paulist Press, 1992), p. 116.

Eckhart on God needing us as much as we need God: *Meister Eckhart: A Modern Translation,* trans. Raymond Bernard Blakney (New York: Harper, 1941), p. 121.

Growing God

Rahner on questioning and infinite possibilities: Karl Rahner, *Foundations of Christian Faith*, trans. William V. Dych (New York: Crossroad, 1989), pp. 32–35.

 CHAPTER 2

"As spirits [we] belong to the eternal world....": C. S. Lewis, *The Screwtape Letters* (New York: Macmillan, 1948), pp. 44, 45.

"He leaves the creature to stand....": C. S. Lewis, *The Screwtape Letters* (New York: Macmillan, 1948), p. 47.

"...simply for the sake of purifying his heart....": John Cassian, *The Twelve Books of the Institutes of the Coenobia*. In *Nicene and Post-Nicene Fathers*, trans. Edgar C. S. Gibson (Peabody, Mass.: Hendrickson, 1994), vol. 11, p. 275.

"...although waiting is *not* having....": Paul Tillich, "Waiting," in *The Shaking of the Foundations* (New York: Charles Scribner's Sons, 1948), p. 151.

Sources

"...there is no need to be troubled....": Fyodor Dostoyevsky, *The Brothers Karamazov*, trans. Constance Garnett (New York: Signet, 1980), p. 69.

CHAPTER 3

"Circuit preachers" and "psychodynamics": Harvey Cox, *The Seduction of the Spirit: The Use and Misuse of People's Religion* (New York: Simon and Schuster, 1973), p. 219.

"God's risk": John Macquarrie, *In Search of Happiness* (New York: Crossroad, 1983), p. 23.

CHAPTER 4

"[T]he world is eaten up by boredom....": Georges Bernanos, *The Diary of a Country Priest*, trans. Pamela Morris (Garden City, N.Y.: Doubleday Image, 1974), p. 2.

"These are thy wonders, Lord of love....": George Herbert, "The Flower," in *The English Poems of George Herbert*, ed. C. A. Patrides (London: Dent, 1984), p. 173.

 CHAPTER 5

"Daily they grow, and daily forth are sent....": Edmund Spenser, *The Faerie Queene, in Edmund Spenser's Poetry*, ed. Hugh Maclean (New York: W. W. Norton, 1968), III.vi.36, p. 273.

"Thanks be to thee....": *Didache*, in *Early Christian Writings*, trans. Maxwell Staniforth (New York: Penguin, 1978), p. 232.

"...men are made for happiness....": Fyodor Dostoyevsky, *The Brothers Karamazov*, trans. Constance Garnett (New York: Signet, 1980), p. 59.

"Christianity is peace, joy, love....": Alden Hatch, *A Man Named John: The Life of Pope John XXIII* (Garden City, N.Y.: Doubleday Image, 1965), p. 166.

Also by Kerry Walters
Published by Paulist Press

Soul Wilderness: A Desert Spirituality

Godlust: Facing the Demonic, Embracing the Divine

Spirituality of the Handmaid: A Model for Contemporary Seekers

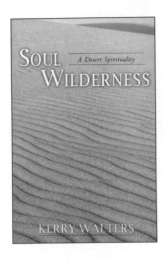

Soul Wilderness

A Desert Spirituality

Kerry Walters

This powerful book draws on the tradition of the prophet emerging from the wasteland to help waken the mystic within each of us, guide our modern spiritual journey into our own inner desert, and there to have a direct experience of God.

"With heart-felt wisdom, Kerry Walters shows how the way of the desert can be a path to freedom and joy, a place where we find our true selves and break through to new life." —*Robert Ellsberg*
Author of *All Saints*

ISBN: 0-8091-4007-1   **Price $12.95**

(Price and availability subject to change)

Ask at your local bookstore.

For more information or to get a free catalog of our publications, contact us at:
Paulist Press • 997 Macarthur Boulevard • Mahwah, NJ 07430
1-800-218-1903 • Fax: 1-800-836-3161
E-mail: info@paulistpress.com • Visit our website at www.paulistpress.com